SIT OPPOSITE EACH OTHER

For David and Hollis

by Hollis Summers

POETRY

Sit Opposite Each Other
The Peddler and Other Domestic Matters
Seven Occasions
Someone Else
The Walks Near Athens

FICTION

The Day After Sunday
The Weather of February
Brighten the Corner
City Limit

SIT OPPOSITE EACH OTHER

HOLLIS SUMMERS

RUTGERS UNIVERSITY PRESS

New Brunswick, New Jersey

The author is grateful for permission to reprint poems which first appeared in the following publications:

American Scholar: The Old Man Over Sherry.

American Weave: I have Learned from Television, and Not Badly, How to Be a Hero.

English Record: This Tarantula; An Old Man in Winter; Lines for Charles; The Visitation; Mercy.

Library News: Biography.

Literary Review: The Lovers; Notes for a Song; Brochure for the Pilgrims.

Midwest Quarterly: Waiting Bench with Figure; The Local Time.

New Mexico Quarterly: Seagull.

New Orleans Review: How To Get Along in the World.

Page: The Local Time.

Penny Papers: For Incanting.

Poems from the Hills—1970: Thruway (© 1970, MHC Publications).

Poetry Northwest: Late 1960s, Winter; The Albums; The Trouble with the Rule of Thumb: I Wear Nine Other Fingers.

Poets on the Platform: Barber; The General; The Separation.

Saturday Review: A Kind of Prayer (© 1968 Saturday Review, Inc.); Tour (© 1970 Saturday Review, Inc.).

Southern Poetry Review: The Accident.

Spectrum: The Richmond Tri-Annual Review: Processional; Rest on the Flight.

Twigs: For a Gallery Goer Admiring a Pottery Heart (© 1967); Striking Clock (© 1967); Anniversary Mass (© 1968); The Pinning (© 1968).

Wormwood Review: More Nuns.

CONTENTS

I

3   If Time Matters

4   The Separation

5   Train

6   The Girls

8   The Fountain

9   Poem

10   On Leda and the Swan

11   Report

12   My Most Interesting Experience

13   At the Museum

14   Matador

15   History

16   Dipper

17   The Roofs

18   More Nuns

20   Seagull

21   For Incanting

22   Brochure for the Pilgrims

24   For a Gallery Goer Admiring a Pottery Heart

25   Flagship, Tourist Class

26   Tour

27   The Professionals

28   Rest on the Flight

29   Sighting

I I

33 Dear Reader

34 How to Read a Newspaper

35 In No Uncertain Words

36 The Conditions

37 The Call

38 Processional

39 Grace

40 Foul Are Unctuous Luckless Kin Nor Eventually Redeemed

41 The General

43 Having Eaten Crow and Invited Company In

44 Dog (Sex, Bone Structure, Nationality)

45 Mercy

47 Counting On

48 Portrait: Of His Liberal Mirror

50 The Actors

51 This Tarantula

52 A Kind of Prayer

53 Paul Siple

54 The Pinning

55 Spectrum

56 Biography

57 Notes for a Song

58 The Relations

59 The Visitation

III

63 How To Get Along in the World

64 Winter Remembrance for the Righteous Feeding Good
        Birds

65 The Trouble with the Rule of Thumb: I Wear Nine
        Other Fingers

66 The Local Time

67 Waiting Bench with Figure

68 The Albums

70 Late 1960s, Winter

71 Thruway

72 The Accident

73 Lines for Charles

74 High School Photograph with Calendar, Courtesy of
        Lamborn's, Athens, Ohio

75 Anniversary Mass

76 Barber

77 I have Learned from Television, and Not Badly, How
        to Be a Hero

78 Leaving

79 An Old Man in Winter

80 The Old Man Over Sherry

81 The Lovers

82 First Snow

83 Vision

84 The Transaction

85 Song for a Dead Lady

86 Striking Clock

87 After the Twelve Days

I

IF TIME MATTERS

If time matters, and of course it does, take a plane;
If time is even more important, go by ship.
Sit in a bar, or a lounge, or a library away
From the elements, anywhere where windows wait
Wide enough to hold your eyes. Choose one window
Holding a sea as tall as a railing,
Twice, three times as tall as a railing,
A window full of sea,
And then a slow becoming window full
Of sky, and sea again, and sky, and sea.
Consider the importance of any small mystery,
A cup of tea, or a piece of paper.
A plane, too, is like a jail,
But it does not hold a place named *Jail*.
Ships do, as truly as does the Vatican.

THE SEPARATION

When riding on trains in any country
When possible—well, it is possible;
Make it possible—arrange to sit opposite
The person you love, taking travel.

One of you views the about to happen
The other what is leaving,
Knowing that if you sat together
You would still make different journeys.

Opposite, two people admit two sceneries.
If, later, seen landscapes become important,
You can try to merge the fields and mountains
Sensing, at least, you have traveled together.

It is possible to make arrangements. I insist
You will need to remember.
I should not need to be telling this.
I should not need to remember.

TRAIN

South of Rome, because of the prevalence of tunnels,
A traveler looks quick and hard:
A train window holds tableaus for a moment
The yellow village turns into a girl
Poised in an orchard, into a Byron mountain,
Into a boat of fishermen hanging on the sea,
Into a beach of rocks, a mist, a goat,
To disappear, only perhaps finally.

Seated south of Rome, among the tunnels,
I have watched the pictures quick and hard.
I have remembered almost all the pictures.

I have not meant to remember the standing man
Who considered his window of scenes from the narrow
     aisle.
He opened the window, as if to let his pictures in.
I was not sure he waited for the longest tunnel.
Rome is a kind of goal for a variety of people.

But whatever he held in his dark hand he threw
Quick and white into the longest darkness.
He disappeared into another compartment
Perhaps, and quite possibly, not forever.

He was young. The half-light turned him old.
It is not necessarily true
Anyone will find
Whatever white the young man threw.

THE GIRLS

I have necessarily moved between them,
Forgetting something at one of the stations,
Returning, to leave something else:
A Bible, a lease, a will, a billfold
Full of identifications and some change,
Returning, forgetting, returning until
I hardly knew which disaster I was leaving from;
And I confess
I used to be equally afraid
Of Scylla and the other one.

I'm still afraid of Scylla,
Her tiny bark and vicious bites.
I will never forget one night with Scylla.
And she still lives in the cave;
Her feet still dangle the air;
Her heads still snatch at monsters and sailors;
She never goes hungry.
But I have finally settled my belongings
Among the other one.
Often, settled, I foget what we used to call her.

The other one does not really suck the straits
And spew them out again—she never did.
That's a legend people tell
To scare compulsive sailors and themselves.
But you shouldn't fault a fellow for making up a story.
Everybody gets comfort from scaring himself and
        making up,
Particularly when Scylla's really true
Dangling her legs and showing her teeth

Waiting.
The other one's name was never Charybdis.

Her name is Carnation.
She mutters
A crinkled froth, like petals.
A fisherman who never did much but fish
Told me her real name.
You can trust a fisherman more than a sailor.
He works in a single territory;
He raises carnations at home;
He never heard a carnation
Called the flower of the dead.

THE FOUNTAIN

She wanted her virginity
Somebody else wanted her virginity
She prayed to a third party
She ran praying
To be a fountain;
She became not only a fountain
But a fresh fountain
Flowing
Flowing
At the edge of the saltiest sea.

Necessarily her fountain
Wanted containing
Nobody wants fresh water
Wasted in brine.

Two islands of papyrus thrive
In her rushing pool
Three ducks swim
Self consciously
Four fish chase each other
And five lean rats
Strong as rapists
Control her waters
Within the pitted boulders
Sporting a frenzy of pink geraniums.

POEM

Clouds
like diagrams for clouds
hang
over among before in through
prepositions come more difficult than verbs
this cold May
the sky

gulls
hang
pointing out the clouds
consider here
there
I have hung cold on the beach for seven days
to make these words.

ON LEDA AND THE SWAN

Now, I've seen most of the paint and stone
Telling of lovely Leda and the lecherous swan;
Now, I've read most of the poems about them—

Not all, of course: we will be seeing more;
Every maker likes to tell a story
Luxuriantly both classical and dirty;

But I know enough to make a summary.
In the words the helpless girl is raped.
If sometimes fluffily, she still is raped.

In paint and stone Leda takes charge.
A pet goose is Jove, Zeus, God.
I think I believe the pictures.

REPORT

Allow me to speak of the great tits
Of Britain, an area I have visited.

They are plump, aggressive, valiant.
The mother is quick to defend her nest.

In three weeks a pair of tits
Will kill seven thousand insects.

They are glorious acrobats,
Hanging in every conceivable position.

I got my word from *The Birds of Britain*
And a three-week walking trip near London.

With a guide, who proved both faithless and faithful,
With my wife, wearing the ridiculous name of June,
The month I was born
(My virtuous mother
Gave me gold pieces for Birthdays and Easters),
With her lover wearing the ridiculous name of Easter,
I, ridiculous, bearing my own name,
Went, in June, to hunt gold, in a jungle, in Africa.

We experienced the whole adventure film:
Drums, spears, boiling pots,
Magic words, potions,
The ministrations of several voodoo men,
And even a native princess
Who was taken by my presence.
I remember a child slipping gold pieces
Against each other, three, five, seven gold pieces.

Always a Master of Ceremonies
Stood in a central hut
Behind a sparkled curtain;
Of course we returned safely.
The child hummed "Tales from the Vienna Woods."
We made many recordings.
We took many pictures.
Chiefly I remember a nursing leopard.

AT THE MUSEUM

Captain Scott wrote in his Journal,
"For God's sake look after our people."

And I have seen the world's largest flower,
Too big for seeing or thinking about.

It took six months for the bud to mature,
A parasite growing on a vine's roots,
A network of threads, like fungus.

In a few days putrefaction began.

I have given up loving.

Love refuses either proof or plan.

"For God's sake look after our people,"
I write in my Journal,

Having looked for an hour
At the world's largest flower.

MATADOR

After a full season of Sundays at five
I know with one unfortunate pass the bull
Finds his fighter's genitals.

I know how all shadows fall at five
Brooding upon the flailing bull.

I have seen a television camera
Linger on a smiling face cold
With smiling, his product sold.

The actor adds a smile to his smile for the camera
Reverencing the camera cold.

HISTORY

After the Greeks, after the Romans,
After the Barbarians came,
They stopped developing carts,
The roads decayed;

For a thousand years of Christians
Mere litters replaced the carts;
Nobody but pilgrims left home,
Knowing no carts but their own feet;

While all the while the other invaders
Waited, conceiving efficient harnesses,
Saddles, stirrups,
And iron horseshoes.

DIPPER

He looks like a stout wren.
His nest is only a miracle,
Like other nests. Like other singers
He sings through half the year
A fairly brilliant trilling warble,
Although the call-note is his usual.
He flies powerful through any air.
He runs particularly well.
Like most British songbirds
His skills are merely normal.

He does not walk on water. That is a rumor.
But consider. Of all those singing fowl,
He, alone, manages water,
Flying for dinner under water.
He runs or flies to plunge
Under water, flying. He propels
Himself, feet and wings aflutter,
Overcoming the evolution of us all.
His name comes from his manners.
He curtsies while sitting still.

Romance aside, but not far aside,
A thatched roof of Norfolk reed

Will last you up to eighty years;
They're durable, if dear.

Count on Devon reed for forty;
Wheat straw, twenty—plenty

Of covering for some to take.
But I recommend you buy Norfolk.

Knowing how Romance means:
Thatching still is done by men

Without machine, although the thatchers
I know live in luxury trailers.

Surely more Baptist than Roger Williams
I am surprised to come upon
Nuns on every single travel.

Today, for instance, four appeared,
With five prancing loud nymphets
In bathing suits of flowered net,
The nuns were habited.

Through my window that looks at the sea
I watched the girls wade out to their knees
Followed by nuns—only three
Through the water, up to their ankles
And even beyond: the fourth nun,
A sandpiper lady, chose to run
Instead of having her picture taken.

Before I could dress and get down to the beach
For a casual stroll the group had finished
A quick picnic of sandwiches,
Potato chips, and Fanta drinks;
They were engaged in a jumping match.
The skittery nun stood and watched.
She also smiled at me, I think.

The girls went out of their matted heads
When the contest dwindled to two of the sisters.
The fatter one was acclaimed the winner.

Once I knew a Baptist lady
A missionary who carefully mothered
Seven daughters, and none considered
Ever becoming a missionary.

SEAGULL

I would not care to touch a common sea gull
From gray and greenbrown spotted egg to full
And final fluttered feather. His obscene call,
That grated *kee-ah*, makes my ears crawl.
I am too delicate to name the smell
Of an offal-feeding gull. And I rebel
Against watching his face or gait. I will,
Naturally, not think of eating one. Until
The gull reaches a different perch in the protocol
Of nature, my knowing senses must extol
Only the non-gull. (But, oh, the white
And pearl perfection of his senseless flight.)

FOR INCANTING

Say in the presence of alyssum and asters,
"Here, once, alyssum and asters grew."
Stand in zinnias and say, "I knew
Zinnias once." Speak carefully in the past
Of present gentians and present four-o'clocks.

Hurry memory among all
September flowers, particularly perennials,
For perennially your mind must walk
Awkward through crying streets where snow
Falls black among your shadow immense
Beyond any moving influence
In the stumbled night. Perhaps you will know,
Admitting the night, that only winter has come.

Perhaps you will know you walk wearing
Only the night, suddenly able to bear
Yellow and white chrysanthemums.

BROCHURE FOR THE PILGRIMS

Those who will join the Pilgrimage
Should send entrance fees with sufficient postage
To cover delivery of Pilgrim Badges
And windscreen slips for advertising.

Every parish may bring its own
Patronal or parochial banner;
Crosses should be left at home,
If needed they can be acquired.

It is to be wished that many groups
Will end their pilgrimage on foot
Arranging for motors to set them down
At the Cock and Bull near the limits of town,

At which point they will embark.
Public conveniences may be found,
As well as ample space for parking,
At the Cattle Market and Festival Grounds.

The Pilgrim's Office, in Town Hall,
As well as the Abbey, will feature stalls
For the purchase of objects of devotion
Including books and other notions.

If vesting arrangements are desired,
Consider vesting in motor coaches,
Joining the Procession north of the church
Where all will be marshalled in groups of four.

The Procession will move to the Abbey nave;
No reverence at the altar will be made;
At every service there will be a collection;
The British Red Cross will be in attendance.

Pilgrims wishing, it is to be hoped,
Details of Services, Litany
Through Evensong, address the Abbey
Enclosing another envelope.

FOR A GALLERY GOER
ADMIRING A POTTERY HEART

We gave each other heart copies
Thrown by our own hands of clay
To recognize and appease
St. Valentine on his day

Unbelieving. They failed to please
The natural red saint. Gray
They settled by degrees
To lumps even we could not say

Resembled hearts. Subject to freeze
And fever still, and decay,
Love's still refugees
Unblessed, we dared not stay

At the shrine of our crumbling hearts to ease
Ourselves with reasons and betray
Our giving. The living witness sees
One heart today. We took away

Our gray shards. Always these
Hearts require rebreaking. They
Require fire, while acquiring this glaze
You, Infidel, praise.

FLAGSHIP, TOURIST CLASS

We walk a great deal when the weather allows,
The women in shoes that look like baked potatoes,
The men in sandals we would scorn at home—
We speak of comfort—but the weather is often foul.

And so we write and talk. We write letters,
In both directions, home and where we go to,
Weaving small webs for holding on;
But our hands cramp and we like talking better.

We always tell each other who we are
At length, describing our homes and where we work
And what we do at Christmas, and our flowers,
And children; and we always say we prefer

Traveling Tourist Class where you get to know
Interesting people, all the while alert
To snatch a glance through the No Admittance doors
Where the opulent, no doubt, also wait for Bingo.

TOUR

Having shot the bus driver
I meant to do away with all the passengers,
Their faces were painted on anyway, under
Expressions named Fear,
Anger, Wonder,
And a couple of Lusts who admired
My cause.

I did a few: a Luster
Who, as he died, kissed his newspaper;
Three Fears, two Angers.
Applause is a pleasure
To any performer.
I ended up with a Wonder
Who failed to join the hearty applause.

I asked everyone to call out his registry number.
They were delighted to cooperate.
I, too, was rather weary.
I drove the bus through the admirable weather
Back to my own borough.
Driving a bus is better than driving a car.
I let out my grateful passengers at their separate houses.

THE PROFESSIONALS

They would have you believe
They are oblivious lovers
Poised in no time, anywhere,
Naked children eating pears.

I am embarrassed to admit this.
I have studied their casualness.
I am sorry their eyes wander
Poised in time, everywhere
As they kiss.

REST ON THE FLIGHT

In those days angels flew everywhere
Bearing messages for travelers:
"Depart another way to your own land,"
And messages for a man who waited
With a woman and a child:
"Arise and flee," "Arise, return,"
"But return to another town."
The air was full of rumors.

Flight takes time.
The people needed rest during their time of flight.
Consider the evenings,
In a landscape of rocks, trees, water,
The child asleep,
Waiting with each other
Quiet in their running
Lighted only by the halos we variously wear.

SIGHTING

We half-danced, half listening to a singer tell
Of a liquid love, when someone, a watcher, shouted
Land. Land was in sight. The band played
To each other, the singer sang to himself.

On deck everyone spoke each other's language.
It was islands, or Portugal, or France, or Spain;
There in the sharp wind, we did not remember
    Geography,
But we agreed on land, saying our names aloud.

In Pomeroy, Ohio, after the water covers
The first Street, Main, and Second,
We return to shore our stores and houses.

In Catania, Sicily, after Etna's black river
Runs clear to the sea; or after the waves of a
    hurricane—
Whatever, there is only one element.

II

DEAR READER

Ever since I used to crouch alone
In the middle of an empty row at The Grand,
In fact, ever since Al Jolson and sound,
I've relished movie musicals
While feeling terribly sorry for the person
Who had to wait, sitting still
While the other person sang and sang.

I kept thinking—I've kept thinking
The scene would be bad enough if it were real.
It would be impossible to sit in your own living room
Listening to a friend or relative sing.
Imagine having your naked face filmed;
Imagine a whole town of lonely people
Watching you pretend to listen.

But the listeners always manage.
Sometimes they do things with their hands
Or teeth or eyelashes; and they pretend well;
And the singer keeps on singing.
I used to wriggle in my middle seat at The Grand
Worrying about the listeners, even though everything
        turned out,
Even though, for all I knew, it was really raining violets.

I still attend musicals. But here's the point.
I've been happier away from them
Sitting in my own living room. Now and then
I've been happier. Listen to me. Listen.
In a minute I'll give you your turn.
I'm trying to take your picture. I'm trying to sing,
Knowing how difficult it is to listen.

33

First, read the headlines;
They never concern you, almost never,
Unless you have, locally, maimed
A child, tattered a jugular,
Committed rape and suicide.
Assume your position sufficiently important to be
        reported.

Consider Death Notes
Until you find a new alien name,
One you never heard once quoted,
Older than you can imagine,
In a town you never ventured;
Read his arrangements: his attitude toward flowers, the
        state of his other kin.

Next, The Stars column,
What it says for your sign and your children's—
Wife and Mother can read their own.
Accept only the compliments,
Ignoring all superstitions
About Romance, Superiors, and relationships with other
        planets.

Gloss through the wonders
Of comic strip children and detectives.
But stay with the words for women:
Festivals, the activities
Of Brunswick stew, of confession,
Among the sweet brides veiled and shining bright with
        their uses for nylon net.

34

IN NO UNCERTAIN WORDS

Everybody knows where my studio is
But late at night nobody ever visits
Over the auditorium where ropes sound
And the wind is a dozen horns.

Last night the door of the broom closet
Next to the piano stood closed.
I always leave it open;
The opening helps what I do to the piano.

Musical sounds came through the door
Like the breathing of rain
Or a potato-chip bag. I called, "Who's there?"
The cellophane stopped and began again.

Who's there? Who is there.
I would have jumped from the arching window
If we had not been on the fifth floor.
Finally I dared to open the door.

A girl sat on a high stool
In a tight sweater eating potato-chips.
Probably she had climbed the sounding ropes
But her breath was as controlled as cold.

She said I was not beautiful.
I watched her posturing shadows.
I spoke to her about the cold.
I have practiced well today.

THE CONDITIONS

Before the Lord demands and insists
You pick up one of those serpents
You'd better think about
How much your chances matter;
You both know He sometimes permits
Bites on your hands and mouth—
Like a man hitting—
When you try to play smart
And do what He wants you to.

If you're a father
You have to trust a kidnaper
To be just a kidnaper,
And the go-between honest,
And your son not bent
On killing himself. Think about it.

It also takes a lot of trust
To be dishonest,
Or be a kidnaper.

THE CALL

On the night of our first wedding
anniversary, we had a party, and the telephone
rang, and a woman, difficult to hear
above everybody's bleared congratulations
said, "My name is Stella.
Your first wife has had a heart attack
and she doesn't love you any more.
My number is 592–1094."

"Stella by Starlight," or is it
"Stella in Starlight?" was our favorite song.
I called my wife. She answered immediately,
my first wife. I asked of her health,
or for it. "I've never felt better,
in my life," she said. "Happy Anniversary."
I have not called Stella in any light,
but I check her name in the directory.

PROCESSIONAL

Did Cinderella really
go to the ball
accoutered, beautiful,

to dance
with a prince
and fall in love to music

we, rejected partners,
in our local finery,
also surely heard;

or did we dream it all
(she was also our step-sister).
Were we really wicked?

GRACE

A trite old woman
And her insanely cured son
Through a casual miracle won
A complete kingdom:

Furnished castle, water,
Food, fire, and, even better,
Laws and an administrator
And his nubile daughter.

They spurned the sinecure
Of course, for everyone prefers
His own old furniture,
His old own manners.

FOUL ARE UNCTUOUS
LUCKLESS KIN
NOR EVENTUALLY REDEEMED

Of course you've heard about Grandmother Byrd
Who can't speak a word since the minister left,

And Cousin Cathleen who went quite off her bean
While quartering Dorene. Indeed we're bereft

As well as sad, for our darling Dad
Has gone as mad as an August dog

And poor little Mother and her half step-brother
Smothered each other by the live oak log.

I'm in such a brown study as I watch the muddy
Water flow Buddy—he was terribly dear—

But how I go on! Dew diamonds the lawn
And someone is rustling the northeast portiere.

THE GENERAL

We were certainly prepared to hold the house,
And most of the world around it,
With ammunition, food, water, conveniences,
Even luxuries, even girls and cigarettes;
And God knows we had drilled:
Every man knew his station;

Our director was the soul of efficiency;
He sat in his scrolled iron chair
Overseeing as gentle and firm
As a story-book general
Where everything is bound to turn out
Not only right but beautiful;

And they attacked on time;
We stood at our places,
In harmony,
The girls sang their rallying chorus;
We were ready for the director's word;
But he did not give his word;

He had moved his chair from the great hall;
He sat in a little study—
Perhaps it was a sewing room—
Flowered wallpaper: green lawn curtains moved at the
        windows;
But the director, in his chair,
Faced away from the windows.

He was polite.
Yes, he knew the time had come.

Yes, he had seen them.
Yes, he heard them now.
Yes, we could be heroes
If we insisted.

Although the whores remonstrated,
We did not insist.
The director was impeached
For a while
And later
Pardoned.

HAVING EATEN CROW
AND INVITED COMPANY IN

I have followed the man who looks like me
Through divers streets and light;
And I have heard men stop
Him often, mistaking him for me,
To ask my answers.

I do not mind the man who looks like me.
He moves ably in the light
Of his disabilities. I will not stop
Following, knowing he will be taken for me
To tell, ask, my answers.

But, Sir, looking like you, look at me.
Stand in the light.
Since my face has changed, stop.
Do you wish to be mistaken for me?
Tell me the questions.

DOG (SEX, BONE STRUCTURE, NATIONALITY)

As surely as dog and master
Turn to look exactly like each other,
Well, so do step-son and father,
Maid and mistress,
Boss and secretary.

And any old people's home holds
A parlorful of siblings.

Listen, you individualist
Mouthing generalities
Already looking no other
Than your dog, master.

MERCY

If you have trouble making arms
Or hands, do not collapse, sculptor;
You can continue your career
Perhaps better without them.

Look at your historical figures.
Look at your family and neighbors.
Who studies the Smiths' knuckles?
Caesar's elbow? Who gives a care?

If you take my advice you can eschew
Both hands and arms; of our eager parts
They ask first to become abstract;
All of our sins and most of our virtues—

Enough for a stunning repertory—
Manage without appendages, a drapery
Here, a muff, a cuff there.
Consider going in for Allegory.

Consider Love or Lust hiding
Arms and hands in flesh,
Gasping, luscious as an actress;
Fancy Charity or Greed

A very labyrinth of pockets;
Faith, Hope, Despair demand
(Oh think of the markets!)
Not a clue of arm or hand.

But Mercy? Who buys it? Mercy
Whose arms not only reach but stretch,
Whose hands adjust to touch,
Mercy was never meant for sculpting.

If you are damned, if you will
Mercy, choose another profession;
Invent a creed, a pill.
Call yourself saint or medicine.

COUNTING ON

Breathing cannot take
All of your time
Take the time to make
A counting rhyme

Count a desk of paper clips
A sidewalk full of cracks
Count a sea awash with ships
The varieties of sex

Count a store of peppers
Count a shore of shells
Count a stack of papers
Count yourselves.

But do not count live stars
Or suns or constant lovers;
Save for wishing on the rare
And painfully discovered.

PORTRAIT: OF HIS LIBERAL MIRROR

In a world where men do
Seven thousand and two hundred
Different kinds of jobs
And dogs are bred to idiocy

He

Fricasseed with money
Liking the utter attention
Of being ostracized

Lives

In a house as gravy gray
As if paint had never been
Invented
Or dogs bred;

His face an oyster
Or a can of seething worms
Wears

Glasses for reading
And closing his eyes behind

Above elevator shoes
Above hard worsteds
Above all

Likes

To say, "As American as baseball,"

Half believing in demons
Angels and other easy myths
Half in analysis

Loathes

The little girls
Who have their pictures taken
Talking to real telephones

And the wet-lipped girls
Proclaiming their betrothals
In every Sunday's news

And all
All
All the Golden Anniversary girls

Goes

Alone to bed in August
Under a coverlet of lace
A dog-faced design

To eat
A variety of meats
Cooked every way
By a Negro woman

Who once served his mother
Who also groaned summer away
Waiting for September
And the end of dog days

The name we give our troubles
Cutting our throats
To fit the cloth
Intricate and beautiful.

Amen.

THE ACTORS

Having played, in *Little Women*, Beth,
As well as countless whores of Hollywood;
Having been Macbeth, Christ, MacHeath;
Having played often publicly together,

What do they consider together both
Waiting in an office, say, of a doctor
Or a judge or a funeral director?
And what do they use for dreams?

They are dumb, the actors;
Thinking other people's words,
Their skeletons sit in other people's manners
Telling us who we are.

THIS TARANTULA

This tarantula walks delicate
Through all our dreams
Shadowing friends and lovers.

He does not need a web
To catch small birds.
He embraces them.

His bite is not fatal.
We can dance our cure
Until we fall.

Taboo means sacred
As well as harmful.

A KIND OF PRAYER

After the bridge falls,
The river moves haunted;
Ferries cover the water
Trembling.

Name the victims,
A cast from B and C movies.
Once the bridge soared
Silver.

Allow what has happened
And kill yourself;
Name what has happened
Stay alive.

Bless the elements,
The investigators,
The cornices of buildings
Waiting to tumble

On a woman entering a shop
A child learning to skip
A man and another man.
Bless the cast.

PAUL SIPLE

So the man who went to the South Pole
As a nineteen-year-old Sea Scout
With Admiral Richard E. Byrd
Is dead. At fifty-nine
His age is fixed.
He kept going back to Antarctica,
I had not known he'd kept going back.
I had forgot his name.

Everybody knew Admiral Byrd was looking for a Scout.
Of course I had not applied, but I was afraid;
I was relieved when Admiral Byrd selected Paul Siple.
I was working on my Tenderfoot badge.
On a wide porch I tied knots
And recited the oath.
The newspaper about Paul Siple smelled sweet.
He lived longer in Antarctica than anyone.

THE PINNING

Recently old and unorganized I attached
Myself alone to a foolish post-puberty rite
From within the spired shadow of a campus church
Although such rites are public, milled with ghosts
Of a thousand formal former lovers watching.

The girls stood among the turgid columns
Of their sorority porch drenched in light
Blouses and full skirts, smiling long
Smiles at the shadow men who darkened the lawn
Lustily singing a tender fraternity song.

Lusty the girls sang a tender song of their own
Swaying their smiles as the night stuttered bright
With standard candles lit by the standard men;
And, behold, two lovers kissed between the lines
Pinned alone, and even I applauded the occasion.

SPECTRUM

Even that foolish girl, who giggling twirls
Batons before her breasts behind her buttocks
Over her head beneath the sky that holds
A rainbow circling this washed April,
Knows color in rainbows no more exists
Than color exists at her feet in the violets
She stamps; an afternoon holds no color at all
Or unreflecting black.

Rainbows mean reflection, refraction, dispersion;
The purple of violets happened eight minutes ago
In the sun; color depends upon the constitution
Of objects. Say it: the angle of reflection
Equals the angle of incidence. Everybody knows:
Perfect flowering colored circles glow
Geometry.
          But I know here with the sun
Violets and rainbow.

BIOGRAPHY

That fall when he was young
He picked up a song for a song
He sang all winter long
And into spring.

But summer stilled his tongue.
He could not pick a song
For wondering at the throng
Of songs to sing.

Still, summer must be sung.
And he was picked for song.
He sings this winter long
Remembering.

NOTES FOR A SONG

I knew wrens built nests,
And produced and reared their chatty young,
And died. I've encouraged them with boxes,
Grasses strung from the arbor,
Food for easy foraging,
Even burial.
             Even that.

But until today, bright as an orange,
A Christmas orange—already our summer
Clothes and faces lie locked
Together far back in the attic—
Until today I never gave a thought
To the practical matters of chickadees,
Their death, or sex, or birth.

I must have assumed they dance our trees
Eternally.
            I have never been caught
With a serious thought on chickadees.
And perhaps I will not, I will not be.

THE RELATIONS

Around the shaggy sun
All the sky staggers
Down Congress Street
Missing none of the houses
Every tree says
Look at me
Nothing relates to anything
Everything says see

THE VISITATION

In the dark room that smelled of mice and crackers
The old man bent to the white paper
Sloshing the matted brush his son had left
Into ink still remarkably liquid;
The old man's voice said, "Birch,"
But his hand with the ink and paper and brush
Said, "Willow"; a willow leaved again,
And the whole room smelled spring.

HOW TO GET ALONG IN THE WORLD

Even should no music sound
Wave to the girl who circles round
And around on a merry-go-round;

Wave to the boy who waits in the back
Of an open truck;

Wave to the man on top
Of any mountain.

They have mounted
On, in, up,
Not because the thing stands,

Not for any reason save
Waving
Being waved to.

Smile and wave.
Say, I have seen you,
I see you.

WINTER REMEMBRANCE
FOR THE RIGHTEOUS
FEEDING GOOD BIRDS

Even if you consider bluejays
Arrogant quarreling thieves
Allow them to attend your feeder;
You can feed them and save
Wrath for causes and other neighbors.
Look slant-eyed. Think color.
Think tropics. Think of a bird
Whose name you never heard.

THE TROUBLE WITH THE RULE OF THUMB:
I WEAR NINE OTHER FINGERS

Or, I could have said
Everybody walks crippled
In St. Paul and Minneapolis;
Or, the trouble with Kansas is
The scenery won't look back at you;
Or, the world is round in Amarillo;
Roads run terra cotta
Through everywhere Georgia;
Santa Barbara is a whore,
Iowa, a dowager,
There's not much sky in Athens, Ohio.

I could have talked a lot about Ohio.
I could have said—I have said—
Mistaking myself for places visited.

THE LOCAL TIME

I am alarmed with television's news
And an international date line;
Therefore I know what happened to tomorrow
In New Zealand. But I am simply undone
With today in Athens, Ohio. I am sick,
Between us,
Of Athens, knowing only a fool abuses
Any place, and determined to resign
Myself with compliments. Truly Athens bestows
Facts better than Greenwich with its Prime Meridian.
Understand, I do not speak against Greenwich, magic
And dangerous
As anywhere. But here in Athens we receive
No public Mean Time. The four faces
Of the courthouse clock stopped long ago bothering
With estimates. Near twelve they stopped cold
And separate, chilled with naming alive or dead
Or slow or fast.

Other watches run generally deceived.
But here, eight times a day, time races
To tell, not knowing exactly we are seeing
Not knowing exactly we are told,
The time. Today the faces said
Long past.

WAITING BENCH WITH FIGURE

The man who sits at the end of the bench is small
Against the sturdy court house of Athens County
Within whose tidily constructed walls,
After the manner of fact, lie
All of our records holding us in thrall
For having committed money, rape, and matrimony.

Make what you will of the mystic public pew
With its seven slats of sufficient height and depth
To put your foot up on to tie your shoe,
Or make a stab at logic, love, and death,
Or wait your wife and taxes coming due.
The man nods, familiar as breath.

THE ALBUMS

Well, hell, I may as well
Tell about the albums
That never got finished.

None of them got finished.

And all the albums spill
Vague unmounted moments
We had meant to paste in:
The small-mouthed squinting aunts
Our asserting parents
Our sons posing as men,
That friend we didn't want—
Which car? Which monument?
Which Christmas? Which April?

Could boys have been so small?
Just look at those lapels.
Remember! Remember?
Why, our town looks foreign.

At least we often smiled.
We smiled among snowmen
As well as daffodils.
Smiling is ritual
In black, white, and color.

We smiled before we died.
How well we look. How well!
Ignore our eyes and hands.

That was a sweet season.
And that. And how we smiled.

And so the pictures lie,
And all the albums tell.
So, well, hell is also
Ordering an album.

LATE 1960s, WINTER

Many Fridays in the last days of the decade
The young—they must have been eighteen—
Danced in Huntington, West Virginia,
Hair in their eyes, to dance on tape again
For Saturday afternoons and television.

More awkward than spastics they swam
The studio air, almost never touching each other,
To the sounds of singers who could not pronounce
Baby, or *love*, or *forever*.
The Announcer, on occasion, gave prizes.

The boys, often broad-bottomed,
Wore billfolds in their tight pants,
Bearing, I suppose, draft cards;
The girls, often small-breasted,
Wore blouses often poorly buttoned.

Making love and dancing and dying
Sometimes, I know, look alike:
I suppose the young watched themselves on television
Watching what they had not known
While snow fell against all our windows.

THRUWAY

We fill all the cold night lanes this December.
We could well drive without any lights
Following our side's four blood ribbons
Confronted by their four blind white.
We move through what is probably countryside.
The lights show us only each other,
Oblongs traveling among some named state.
For a long while it is always winter.

The car is hot, but do not turn off the heater.
Sometimes the red or white strings tatter.
We straighten out. I think our side
Wins. We'll get there surely earlier.
But, listen. Are you listening, white?
Were we unhappy where we were?
Were you unhappy where we want to get?
We must all drive faster together.

THE ACCIDENT

I believe the world was made by God
In the year Six Thousand B.C.,
Through the first six days of January,
And on the Seventh Day He rested.

I believe Adam and the animals
Rose from earth, an immediate act
To be forever fixed, unchangeable fact.
I believe in all recorded miracles.

An airplane falls like a sparrow,
Counted surely. The world is complete.
What else should I believe
Now?

LINES FOR CHARLES

Before rain
The leaves of the tulip tree
Quarrel with each other;
Lightning blooms the horizon
To promise another death
Or growth or graph
Of the man
Standing at the window
Watching
The promises of rain.

Let me stand no different from any day's stance,
Waiting for the mail, or tomorrow;
Let me breathe no deeper than remembering requires;
Let me speak no louder than an average breath saying,
    "Hello,"
Our total love, our sorrow.

HIGH SCHOOL PHOTOGRAPH WITH CALENDAR, COURTESY OF LAMBORN'S, ATHENS, OHIO

I can't tell you,
But I'll try:
This is the business of a poem,
Trying to tell what you can't.

His face waits vulnerable.
Vulnerable is the right word for a calendar.

Time will happen to his calendar.

I wish him healths.
This is a dangerous poem.

ANNIVERSARY MASS

Again today the man has died on the screen,
And lived and died and lived again.
Surely the man is dead now.
An altar rose like Disneyland
Shadow priests marched and bowed,
The man is surely dead now.

Introit, Collect, Epistle, Gradual,
Sequence: language, be merciful.

I cannot hear the wrenched words
Lost in translations I have heard
No more than I have heard the original.
Hear me, words.

I celebrate this mass, dumb;
I call the man who has come
To death and life merciful.

Name the day mercy
We measure time from,
Lord, be mercy, Christ, have mercy.

BARBER

And so I will not go again to the old barber
Whose old fingers tremble;
Although I wish him well
I am concerned with my own skull
And all of the faces I have willingly worn;
I wish him utterly well,
But I will not go again.

And, therefore, I will stop using an electric razor,
Having relished the luxury of myself willing
Battery operation and the unutterable comfort
Of walking around the house and around the yard
Shedding my animal hair without a mirror—
Although I hold little against Sunbeams
Or Remingtons.

It is time I returned to the naked blade
And the strop and the mirror
Employed by my long dead grandfather;
It is time, as well as I am able,
To consider my mirrored face capable
Still of all the lines,
All the blood.

I HAVE LEARNED FROM TELEVISION, AND NOT BADLY, HOW TO BE A HERO

Heroes almost always move
In shadows through a hall
Thinking brotherhood or love
While saxophones call

Above the sound of hearty drums.
The heroes pause at corners
To breathe and check their various arms.
Their cameras blur

Before the doors whose handles wave.
They enter tall and willing
In order to give or take or trade
A kiss, a killing.

LEAVING

Falling like stars or bells
Because they are shaped to fall
They still fall well.

Still leaf-shaped means
Nothing to the man
Who has never seen

Poplar leafed heads,
White oak hands,
Judas tree hearts.

AN OLD MAN IN WINTER

And now the needle of his memory
Skips his whole old age,
All of the grooves of an adequate marriage,
And us, his children, foraging
Here in time,
Assuming seasons
And reasons for seasons.
He listens from another century
Selecting time.

How can we ever shout him back
Here to where we are?
We have called until we can not hear,
We can almost not remember
Here in time.
He walks a road in spring
Singing
With a pail of his mother's biscuits
In time, in his hand.

THE OLD MAN OVER SHERRY

Early in some other century
Once I attended an elegant party
Where fifty men played violins,
And a small lady fluttered a fan.
We danced among the violins.
The lady was full of charity.

Why do I mention the party here
In winter, where no fan moves the air
And my heart is better ordered
And my head clear?
Well, only because I remember
I remember.

THE LOVERS

I like to watch a couple walk
The clear air of Woodward Hill
Up or down, changing the shadows
Of such imponderables as walls,
Or trees, with only their own sustaining shadows.

Sometimes, in and out of sun,
The walking shadows turn to run
Together. What watcher dares for reasons?
But watching, shadowed, I know well
The man and woman color the air they run.

FIRST SNOW

The snow, only a pretend snow, fell up
As much as down, barely covering the sidewalk,
Leaving the grass and the copper chrysanthemums
The color they held yesterday,
Only filming, barely filming, the world.

But our boys, with morning, rose hilarious,
Zippering themselves into all, all of their clothes;
They rolled on the grass by the chrysanthemums;
They said they would build a snowman;
And, for all practical purposes, they did.

VISION

I suppose it is well to travel
Into caves and up to palaces
To study mosaics and frescoes
Mapped with scars and fissures,
Although most of the pictures
Shine more remarkable
In photographs studied at home
Where fissures become lines
And scars disappear
And the eye of faith is not required—
Although faces still appear in the texture
Of your own puckered linens.

THE TRANSACTION

Formerly not really believing in love—
That story is too long to tell—
I have sold blood and sperm:
I would, no doubt, have given them away,
Were a system not established
At all the banks;
And, I have, also, already produced
Breathing and children
On my own.

I had not expected to brood upon
My former transactions.

But today—it is a long story—
I missed both my bank appointments.

I have raced all our streets,
Saying, "Man," "Woman,"
To men and women,
Saying, "Child,"
To Children.

I do not imagine I will sell or even
Give again.

SONG FOR A DEAD LADY

Having mourned both friends and enemies
I am glad to sing an elegy
For a woman who never inspired care
Of foes, lovers,
Neighbors, particularly neighbors.
Her part of me
Dropped into the sea
Needed losing.
It is good she is dead.

There.
I hear what I have said.

But I had to live a long time
To say this song.

STRIKING CLOCK

Forgetting to count the numbers I have heard
The town clock strike, and wanting the time,
Perhaps because I have often heard the same
Time or time is also time remembered,
I have been able to recall the absent numbers.

I am moved by clocks. I would not exaggerate
The importance of an unimportant state
Or gift for all I know all men share;
But surely my words must try to celebrate
Sounds my ear can never hear.

e birds moved so brilliantly
: were never sure of their number
 we assume the tree secured
oroximately twenty-three;
e top of the pear blossomed the partridge
e cooing doves and the colly birds
ttering to find their anchorage
to illustrate they were honestly stirred

the music of fiddles and pipes and drums;
covering among the lower branches
e facts of music and varying stances
nced the hens and geese and swans.

: were always sure of the number of people
: counted together again and again;
neteen women and thirty-one men,
agile as birds but rather more stable,
ying and dancing through gracious progressions,
gant ladies, fiddlers, pipers,
: drummers, the maids who recalled their profession
ly by carrying pails of silver.

 knowing that arms and limbs, like wings,
form their music not forever,
e of the couples gathered together
d blessed themselves with the five gold rings.

e forty remaining continued their play
til the ladies wholly succumbed
the notes of the men who piped and drummed.

87

The dozen fiddlers wandered away
For other pastures and other reliefs.
The birds had gone when the music stopped.
The tree was bare of movement except
For the leaves and the fruit and again the leaves.